Falkland Islands, A Penguin's World
Published by Design In Nature, Falkland Islands

Photography, text and design by Ian & Georgina
Strange, Design In Nature, Falkland Islands

Printed by Butler,Tanner and Dennis Ltd

ISBN   978-0-9550708-2-2

Photo on inside cover © Dan Birch
wwwdanbirchphoto.com : Gentoo penguins on
Steeple Jason Island

DESIGN IN NATURE ®

www.designinnature.com

Falkland Islands

A Penguin's World

Contents

Introduction

Just over half a mile from where we live and the house where most of our studies on penguins are recorded is a large colony of Rockhopper penguins mixed with other seabirds. With certain conditions we can hear and smell this rookery. In the distance we can also see a colony of Gentoo penguins, and virtually on the doorstep there are the burrows of Magellanic penguins. This is New Island, a small, remote island in the far west of the Falkland archipelago.

Since 1972 the island has been operated as a wildlife reserve and here we founded the New Island Conservation Trust. This now ensures the protection of the reserve in perpetuity and its continuation as a centre for field studies into penguin conservation. There are eighteen species of penguin found in the world and although confined to the Southern Hemisphere, they breed in a range of environments from the sub tropical Galapagos Islands, through temperate and sub-antarctic regions to Antarctica. The Falkland Islands are unique in the distribution of these birds, in that six species of penguin breed in the Islands.

This work portrays these penguins and the birds and mammals that are closely associated with them. These form part of the *penguin's world* when these flightless seabirds come to land to breed. Some simply nest in harmony alongside the penguins for reasons that are not clear. For other species, the colonies of penguins are a rich source of feed, either for scavenging waste food brought ashore by the penguins, or for those birds and mammals that prey on the penguins, their eggs or young.

photo : Nesting Rockhopper penguins, cormorants and albatross at New Island's settlement rookery

Rockhopper Penguin Eudyptes chrysocome

In the austral spring month of October the Rockhopper penguins return from migration to their breeding grounds after wintering at sea for six months. Large numbers form colonies at selected sites on some of the Falklands' most formidable rocky coastlines. Nesting alongside such species as the Black-browed albatross and King cormorants, these sites may be many meters above sea level, requiring these small penguins, the smallest of the Islands' penguins, to climb or rock-hop up the most arduous routes in order to reach their nesting places.

A clutch of two eggs is laid in early November and incubated for just over a month. Parent birds forage for food at sea, often travelling hundreds of miles off-shore in search of krill, squid and small fishes. In colonies of several thousands, these small but incredibly resilient penguins will raise their chicks, until the time comes for their long migration to begin again in March.

photos : Rockhopper penguins often face rough seas as they come ashore from foraging trips. Thick beds of kelp seaweed present formidable barriers too, but little deters these determined penguins from making a landing.

Once they are ashore, Rockhopper penguins face more obstacles as they commence their journey to their breeding sites. Expert climbers, Rockhoppers scramble up boulders and rocky slopes using their strong claws - deep grooves eventually form in the rocks where penguins have passed for hundreds of years.

photos : (far left) Rockhoppers making their way to and from their rookery, passing by nesting Black-browed albatross; (left) Rockhoppers gathered at the base of the steep gully they must climb to reach their nests.

Rockhopper penguins usually breed in colonies together with other seabirds. On New Island they nest alongside Black-browed albatross and King cormorants (opposite page).

Rockhoppers pair for life, returning to the same breeding site each year. Together they call loudly, throwing their heads from side to side in a display of their partnership (left).

These mixed and sometimes huge colonies containing many tens of thousands of nesting birds are a large potential food source for scavenging birds such as Dolphin gulls and Skuas, and the predatory Striated Caracara (pictured right). These birds often breed in close proximity to the seabird colonies, taking the eggs, chicks and discarded feed of the penguins, albatross and cormorants to feed to their own young.

Pictured left is part of the spectacular seabird colony on Beauchêne Island, where tens of thousands of albatross gather each year to breed, and in amongst them nest the Rockhopper penguins.

photos : (above) Scavengers and predators - a Falkland Skua and chick, nesting Dolphin Gulls, and a Striated Caracara with her chicks; (opposite page) A Striated Caracara stealing an egg from a Rockhopper penguin.

Rockhopper penguins lay two eggs, which they incubate for about 33 days, but often they only manage to raise one chick to fledgling stage. The penguin chicks are fed each day on a rich diet of fish, squid and krill. The two chicks in the photo opposite are chasing their parent through the colony of nesting albatross, calling for food.

The chicks are left at the colony in crèches once they are large enough not to be preyed upon by caracaras and skuas, and both of the adult penguins make daily trips to sea to catch and bring back food for their young. About two and a half months after hatching, the penguin chicks will have grown their waterproof feathers and will be ready to leave for the ocean themselves. They will remain at sea for nearly ten months, before returning in the summer to the rookery where they were hatched.

The breeding season over and their young already departed on migration, the adult Rockhopper penguins spend a short period at sea feeding up. They then return to their breeding sites to moult. After moulting they make a final journey to the sea for that season. Following deeply scored routes, formed by the passage of penguins for a thousand years or more, they leave land and commence their seasonal migration.

Even at sea they will follow specific routes, probably marked by variations in the ocean, such as salinity, temperature, tides, light and darkness. After some seven months at sea they will return to their colonies to start a new breeding season.

Macaroni Penguin Eudyptes chrysolophus

The Macaroni penguin is similar to the Rockhopper penguin in several ways, and although it's not commonly found breeding in the Falkland Islands, the Macaroni occasionally makes its home amongst the smaller Rockhopper penguin. In the Falklands, the Macaroni penguin has been known to inter-breed with Rockhoppers.

Bigger and more robust than the Rockhopper, the Macaroni penguin has a more distinct and impressive yellow crest of feathers, a larger bill and a noticeably different call. Their breeding cycle is similar to the Rockhopper's, but little is known about their winter migration from the Falkland Islands - it's likely that these penguins travel up the coast of South America, possibly as far north as Uruguay and Brazil.

Royal Penguin Eudyptes chrysolophus schlegeli

The Royal penguin is a sub-species, and is very similar in appearance to its close relative, the Macaroni penguin, only larger, with a white to grey chin and a heavier bill.

The Royal penguin is endemic to Macquarie Island, (just off the Antarctic Convergence, and lying south of New Zealand), but this striking looking penguin has been recorded breeding in very small numbers in the Falkland Islands. Here, they lay only one egg and have a slightly later breeding season than the Macaroni and Rockhopper penguins.

Photo : Royal penguin with a Macaroni showing size difference (right)

Gentoo Penguin Pygoscelis papua

The Gentoo penguin differs quite significantly from the crested penguins, such as the Rockhopper and Macaroni found in the Falklands. As well as in their appearance, these penguins differ in their behavioural and breeding habits.

The Gentoo penguin is the only Falkland penguin species which is resident in the Islands all the year round. They may make short migration trips in winter, but remain in the Falkland archipelago.

Gentoos congregate in large colonies of several thousands, made up of smaller groups of nesting pairs which can be anywhere from a few to several hundred. It is quite usual that these penguins will move breeding sites by a few hundred meters each season, building new nests on fresh ground.

photos : Gentoos on New Island (left) & Steeple Jason Island (right)

photos : Gentoo penguins usually land on the more accessible beaches, literally surfing the waves ashore and frequently landing on their bellies.

Gentoos appear to prefer sandy
beaches to make their landings from
the sea. Unlike the crested penguins,
they nest in close groups on low lying
coastal heath or grassland and may
nest a kilometer or more from their
coastal landing spots, making the long
walk each day to go to sea and feed.

In the process of nest-building Gentoo penguins may strip bare all the vegetation on a breeding ground. In turn these sites receive a dressing of excreta rich in phosphates and nitrogen. As the penguins move to new nesting sites, so the old breeding grounds regenerate with a new cover of rich vegetation.

photos : (far left) Gentoos in a scenic nesting spot beneath Queen Victoria cliff on New Island. Note the ground devoid of vegetation, but white from the penguins excreta; (left) An adult Gentoo penguin making a display call

photo : At the northern end of New Island, Gentoo penguins make their nests in an idyllic location, coming and going from the sea on the wide sandy beach at the head of the bay.

photos : (above) Nest-building and breeding begins in late September and two eggs are laid in mid to late October. Chicks hatch after 33-34 days of incubation.

In the Falkland Islands, Gentoo penguins often successfully raise two chicks. The chicks are cared for by their parents, being fed regurgitated Lobster krill, schooling fish and squid. Gentoo chicks grow rapidly, and by mid January they are left in crèches, being looked after by just a few adult birds. This allows both of the parents to go to sea and find enough food for their young. Gentoos generally do not travel great distances to catch most of their food, remaining fairly close to their breeding sites, making only short trips. By late February to early March, the young penguins will be ready to go to sea for the first time to find food for themselves.

photos : Each evening during the breeding season, Gentoo penguins arrive back from their foraging trips at sea, with bellies full of food to give to their chicks. Even though these penguins often move to new nesting sites, they continue to use the same path to and from the coast, creating a well-worn "penguin highway".

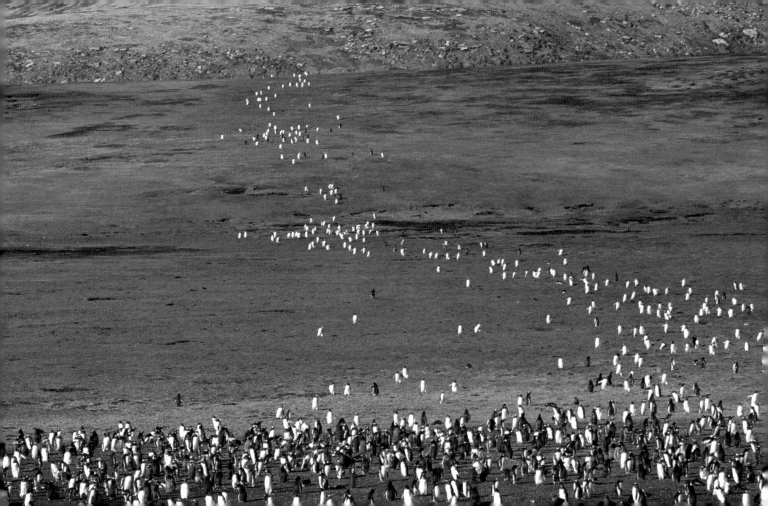

A rare bird of prey, the Striated Caracara, or "Johnny Rook" (left), relies heavily on penguin colonies for food. In the Falkland Islands, Johnny Rooks prey and scavenge on the eggs and chicks of Rockhopper and Gentoo penguins during the breeding season. In the winter months, the non-migratory Gentoos provide an important source of food for the Caracara. Early voyagers to the Islands referred to the Gentoo penguins as "Johnny penguins" - the Caracara's rook-like appearance and their close association with these penguins earned them the name of Johnny Rook. Similarly, Rockhopper penguins were often nicknamed "Jumping Jacks", and the Caracara also known as "Jack Rook".

In late February as the Gentoo breeding season is closing, the colonies start to disperse with the fully fledged young moving closer to the sea in preparation for leaving. Birds may then vacate their usual breeding sites to make short migration trips within the archipelago. It is possible that this is carried out to allow breeding sites to weather and clean off. At such times Gentoos may come ashore to rest in non-breeding site areas.

Photo : (right) A scene at Penguin Point near Deaths Head on the mainland of West Falkland

Magellanic Penguin *Spheniscus magellanicus*

Magellanic penguins are unique among the Falkland penguin species, in that they live and nest in burrows underground, usually beneath Tussac grass pedestals.

These penguins have a very distinct braying call, which sounds similar to that of a donkey, and hence they are locally nicknamed "Jackass" penguins. In the evenings when these birds come back to their burrows, the air is filled with the sound of their calls, as they wait for their partners to return to the nest.

Magellanic penguins are widely distributed, being found on many offshore Tussac islands in the Falklands. Large populations also exist on the north and north-east coasts of mainland East Falkland, but since the introduction of grazing stock such as sheep and cattle, there has been a significant loss of Tussac grass, and so here, the penguins form their burrows on the coastal heath and grasslands.

photos : (left) Two nearly fledged Magellanic chicks with an adult; (right) A Magellanic calls in the late evening from the entrance of its burrow, beneath a Tussac grass pedestal.

Magellanic penguins lay a clutch of two eggs in mid October, and incubate them for about 40 days. The chicks are reared inside the burrows until mid to late January. As the chicks grow older they venture just outside the entrance of their burrows, but normally accompanied by one of the parent birds.

During the breeding season adults forage at sea, and like the Gentoos, they generally stay within a range of some 40 miles offshore, feeding mainly on small schooling fishes and squid.

photos : (left) With an adult penguin amongst Sand grass and Sheep's Sorrel, two Magellanic chicks with the last of their downy feathers; (right) An adult pair of Magellanics

Unlike Rockhopper and Gentoo penguins the eggs and young of Magellanic penguins are less vulnerable to predation by Striated Caracara and skuas due to their habit of nesting in burrows underground. However, Southern Sea Lions (right), will sometimes predate on the different species of penguin found in the Islands.

This predation, which is considered abnormal for this species of seal, usually occurs as penguins are about to land, although in the case of Magellanic penguins, Sea Lions will sometimes catch them as they make their way inland through the Tussac grass to their burrows.

By the end of January, Magellanic chicks are fully fledged and will start to leave their burrows and head for the sea for migration north.

The adult penguins moult in March, and then leave their breeding sites, following the same northern migration pattern, up the coast of South America, often as far north as Brazil.

King Penguin Aptenodytes p. patagonica

The largest of all of the Falkland penguin species, and second largest in the world to the Emperor penguin, King penguins stand at about 76cm tall and have a striking plumage with their golden-orange auricular patches and steely blue-grey feathers.

The Falkland Islands present the most northerly range of the King penguin - though it is a far less common breeder in the Islands than the Rockhopper, Magellanic or Gentoo penguin species. However, there is clear evidence that the King penguin is increasing in numbers in the Falklands, with new breeding sites being established.

King penguins are highly gregarious, and in the Falklands they are often associated with colonies of Gentoo penguins and may breed in small numbers in amongst them. Kings also prefer the type of breeding habitat that Gentoo penguins select, with sandy beaches as an easy access to and from the sea.

The King penguin has a unique breeding cycle amongst the penguin species found here, laying only one egg and incubating it for around 55 days.

Unlike other Falkland species of penguin, individual breeding pairs are not synchronous with each other, and therefore within a single colony it's possible to find birds with eggs, some with chicks, and others with grown young, as well as immature and moulting birds at the same time.

During courtship the King penguin performs an impressive ritual of bowing and "trumpeting", where birds stretch to their full height and call, displaying to their partners.

The chick-rearing and breeding cycle of the King is very much longer than other penguins, taking approximately 10 to 11 months to complete in the Falklands. In its more southerly breeding areas, this cycle may take over 12 months.

69

photos : King penguins during courtship and mating

The earliest that the King penguin's courtship and egg-laying may take place is early to mid November. A pair commencing their cycle at this time will be later the following season, and by the third season this breeding cycle may be too late to start due to the approach of the winter.

March is the beginning of fall in the Falklands and late for birds to commence breeding. A pair reaching this stage will therefore take time out from breeding and recommence their cycle in the spring, occasionally resulting in a pair losing a breeding season.

photos : King penguins in Falkland winter-time. At this stage, King penguin chicks have such thick downy feathers that they often look bigger than the adult birds.

About our work & this book...

A Penguin's World is not only a collection of photographs, but a portrayal of the penguin's reality - the world that they live in, and one that they share with us. We wanted to show their beauty, their special nature and how unbelievably resilient they really are. Although this book is specific to the Falkland Islands and the penguins which are found here, it pays homage to all of the penguin species found world-wide, as they really are remarkable birds.

On New Island, a remote nature reserve in the Falkland Islands, where we live and where most of this work is based, our penguin species are protected - but the place where these penguins spend most of their lives, the marine environment on which they depend is not fully protected. Commercial fishing , pollution and changes in sea temperatures are all potential threats to these birds. On New Island, through scientific research, we are working towards a greater understanding of the penguin's ecology and in particular, the significance of changes in their marine environment.

We hope that by sharing some of the penguin's world that we know with you, you will gain an insight into what it's like to live alongside these amazing birds.

Ian & Georgina Strange, Design In Nature 2009   www.designinnature.com / www.newislandtrust.com

Ian & Georgina Strange are a father and daughter team, working together as photographers, designers and publishers under "Design In Nature" in the Falkland Islands. A Penguin's World is their third joint publication, with eight books on the Falkland Islands previously authored by Ian Strange, a well known naturalist.

Acknowledgements & Dedication

The images in this work are the result of years of photographing in different parts of the Falklands. We extend our thanks to friends and especially landowners who made this possible.

Thanks go to Dan Birch, Deborah Scott and Maria for their imput, proofing and comments, etc.

Finally, this work is dedicated to all those who have worked on wildlife, in particular penguins on New Island and the continuation of this island as a reserve in perpetuity under the protection of the New Island Conservation Trust.

Ian & Georgina Strange
New Island
Falkland Islands